The Hand book

Albatros

The hand is THE TOOL of tools

Aristotle (philosopher)

Hands...

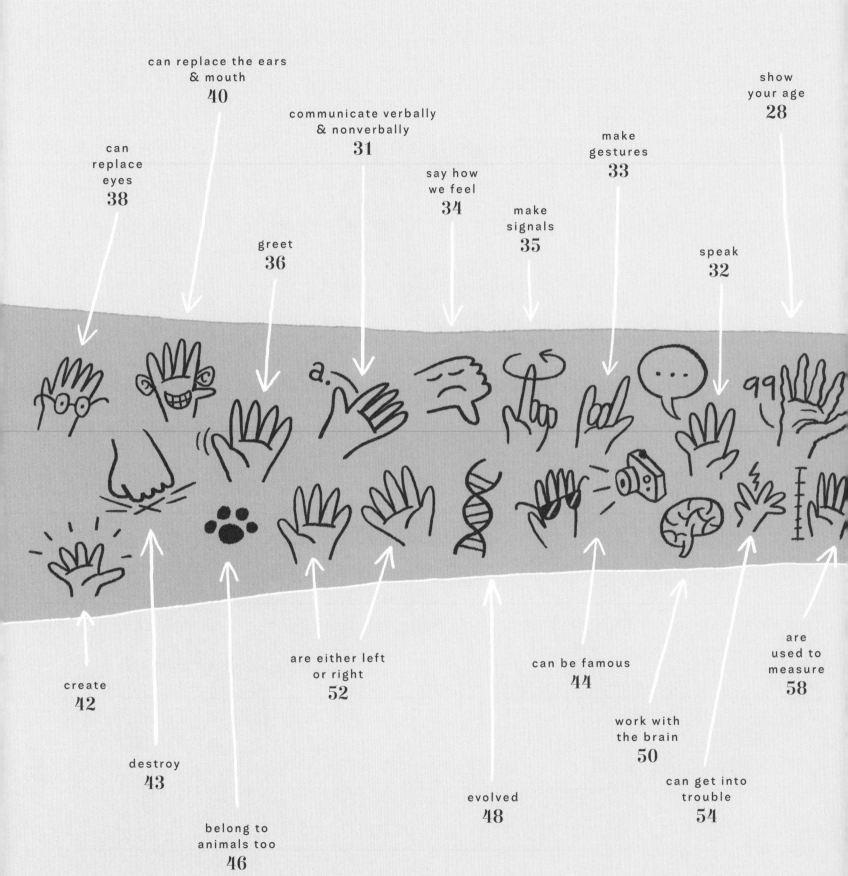

can replace the ears
& mouth
40

communicate verbally
& nonverbally
31

show
your age
28

can
replace
eyes
38

say how
we feel
34

make
gestures
33

make
signals
35

speak
32

greet
36

create
42

are either left
or right
52

can be famous
44

are
used to
measure
58

destroy
43

work with
the brain
50

can get into
trouble
54

evolved
48

belong to
animals too
46

touch
25

feel &
recognize
26

give &
cooperate
23

are unique
12

leave
fingerprints
14

rest
24

can do many
things
20

hold
22

communicate
30

have
anatomies
16

BLAH

can use sticks
68

can have rings
& accessories
66

have different
professions
56

can get
injured
70

can be
replaced
72

can be
decorated
64

shouldn't
do certain
things
76

are
symbols
60

need good
hygiene
75

get
depicted
62

glossary
9

Glossary

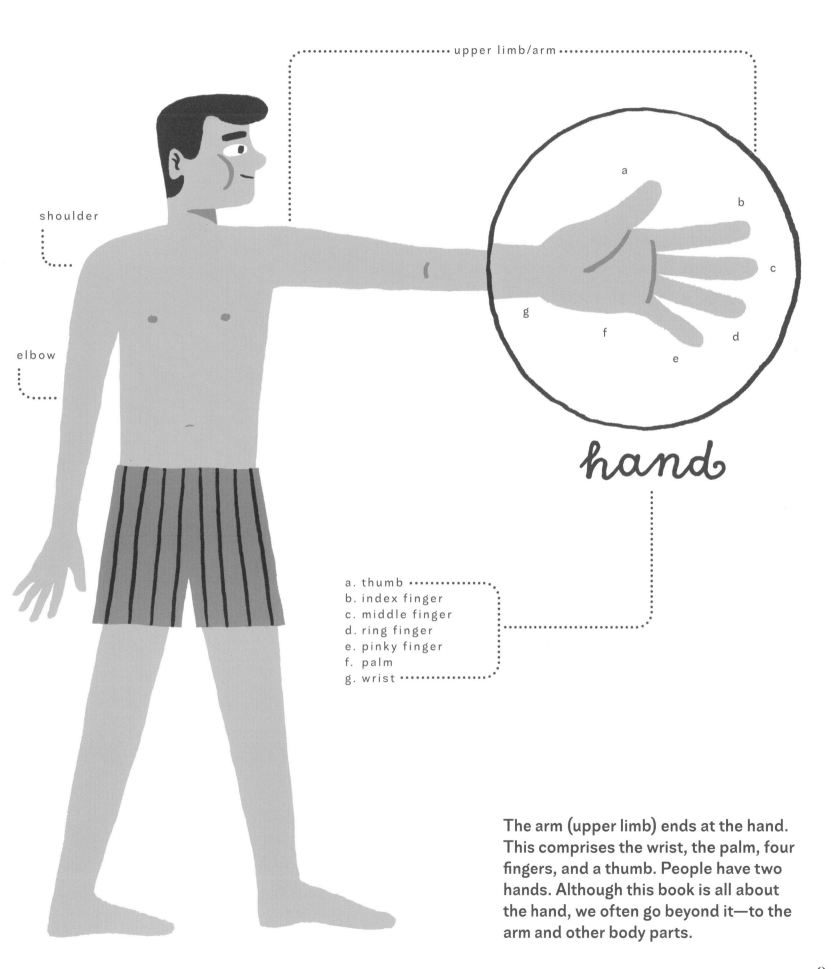

upper limb/arm

shoulder

elbow

hand

a. thumb
b. index finger
c. middle finger
d. ring finger
e. pinky finger
f. palm
g. wrist

The arm (upper limb) ends at the hand. This comprises the wrist, the palm, four fingers, and a thumb. People have two hands. Although this book is all about the hand, we often go beyond it—to the arm and other body parts.

hand with
fingers
outstretched

dirty hand

fingerless hand

thin-fingered
hand

square hand

clumsy hand

hand
in a cast

hairy hand

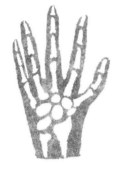
X-rayed hand

At first glance, all hands look the same.

wooden
hand

bony hand

invisible hand

hand in glove

kid
hand

swollen hand

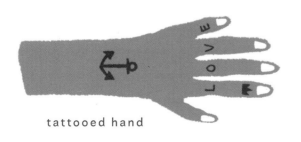
tattooed hand

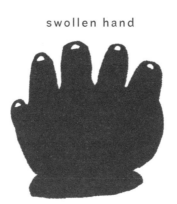

fat-fingered hand

10

scarred
hand

wet hand

giant hand

hand with
bitten nails

adult
hand

dry hand

work-worn hand

sweaty hand

hidden hand

cuffed hand

But are they really?

hand with
painted fingernails

hand shrine

ringed hand

printed hand

hand with
goosebumps

pocketed hand

water-soaked
hand

bruised
hand

pointing hand

Hands are

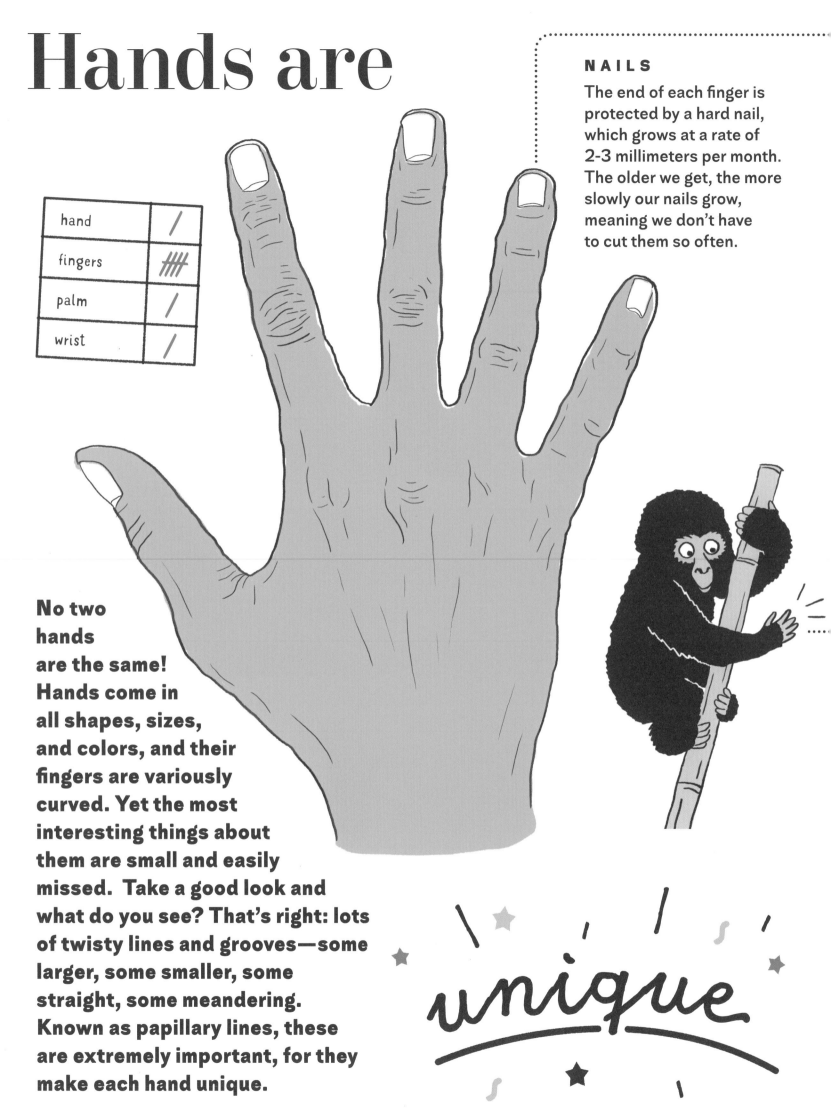

hand	/
fingers	//// (tally of 5)
palm	/
wrist	/

NAILS
The end of each finger is protected by a hard nail, which grows at a rate of 2-3 millimeters per month. The older we get, the more slowly our nails grow, meaning we don't have to cut them so often.

No two hands are the same! Hands come in all shapes, sizes, and colors, and their fingers are variously curved. Yet the most interesting things about them are small and easily missed. Take a good look and what do you see? That's right: lots of twisty lines and grooves—some larger, some smaller, some straight, some meandering. Known as papillary lines, these are extremely important, for they make each hand unique.

unique

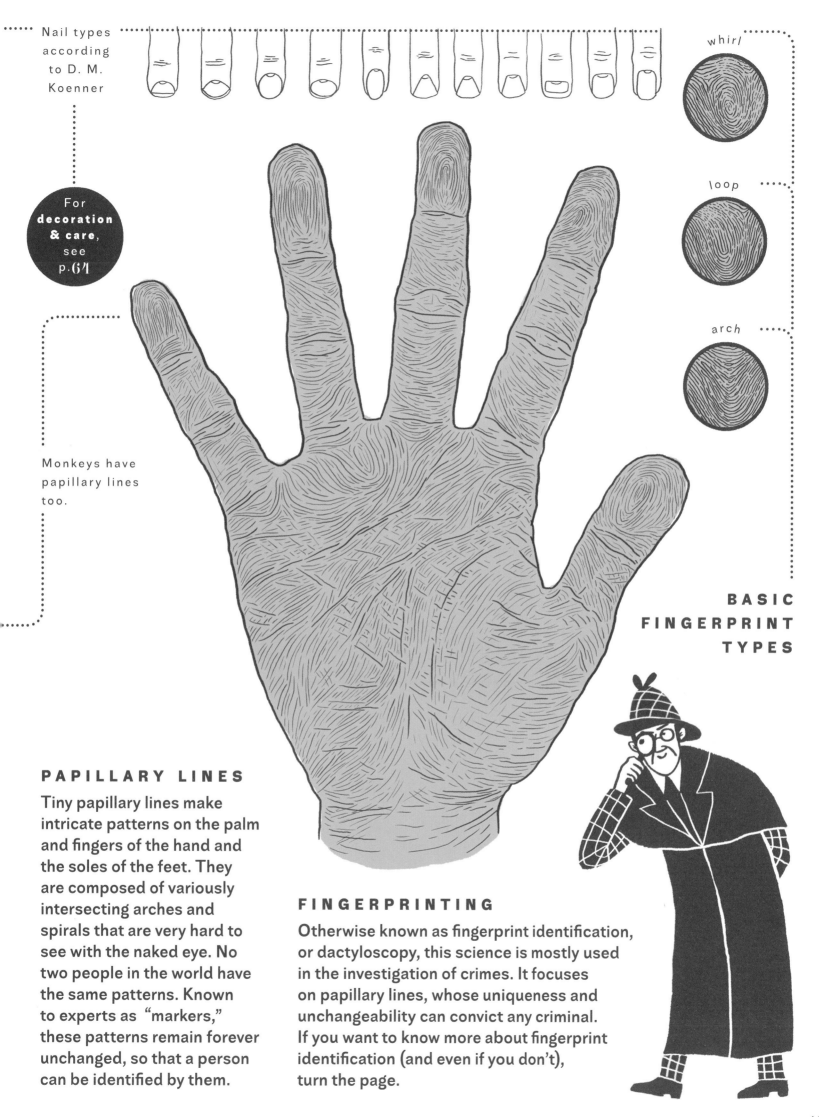

Nail types according to D. M. Koenner

whirl

loop

arch

For **decoration & care**, see p. 64

Monkeys have papillary lines too.

BASIC FINGERPRINT TYPES

PAPILLARY LINES

Tiny papillary lines make intricate patterns on the palm and fingers of the hand and the soles of the feet. They are composed of variously intersecting arches and spirals that are very hard to see with the naked eye. No two people in the world have the same patterns. Known to experts as "markers," these patterns remain forever unchanged, so that a person can be identified by them.

FINGERPRINTING

Otherwise known as fingerprint identification, or dactyloscopy, this science is mostly used in the investigation of crimes. It focuses on papillary lines, whose uniqueness and unchangeability can convict any criminal. If you want to know more about fingerprint identification (and even if you don't), turn the page.

13

INTRIGUE AT A CRIME SCENE
Dactyloscopy

Inside the hand

The hand is a very complex, perfectly functioning mechanism. Each of its parts has its own clearly defined task. For a hand to work as it should, its components must work together. These components are:

joints & ligaments

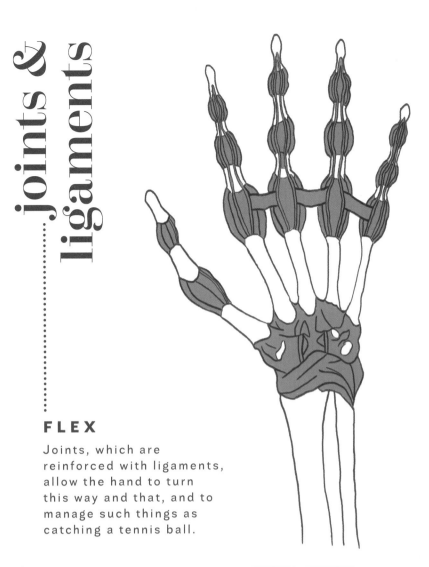

FLEX

Joints, which are reinforced with ligaments, allow the hand to turn this way and that, and to manage such things as catching a tennis ball.

bones

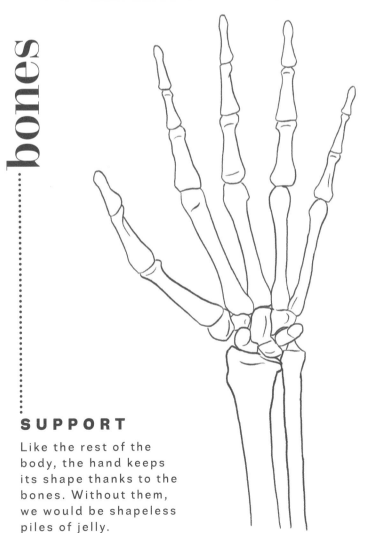

SUPPORT

Like the rest of the body, the hand keeps its shape thanks to the bones. Without them, we would be shapeless piles of jelly.

muscles & tendons

MOVE

Muscles are attached to bones by tendons. As they contract and relax, they cause the hand to move.

blood vessels

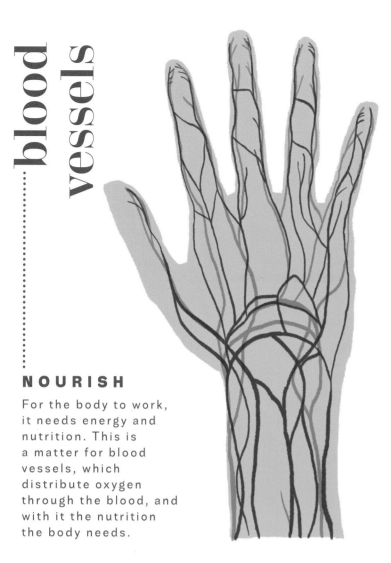

NOURISH

For the body to work, it needs energy and nutrition. This is a matter for blood vessels, which distribute oxygen through the blood, and with it the nutrition the body needs.

nerves

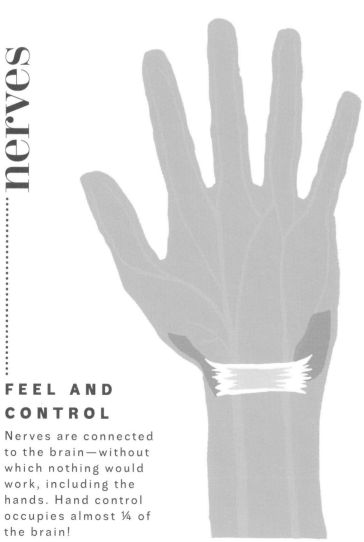

FEEL AND CONTROL

Nerves are connected to the brain—without which nothing would work, including the hands. Hand control occupies almost ¼ of the brain!

skin

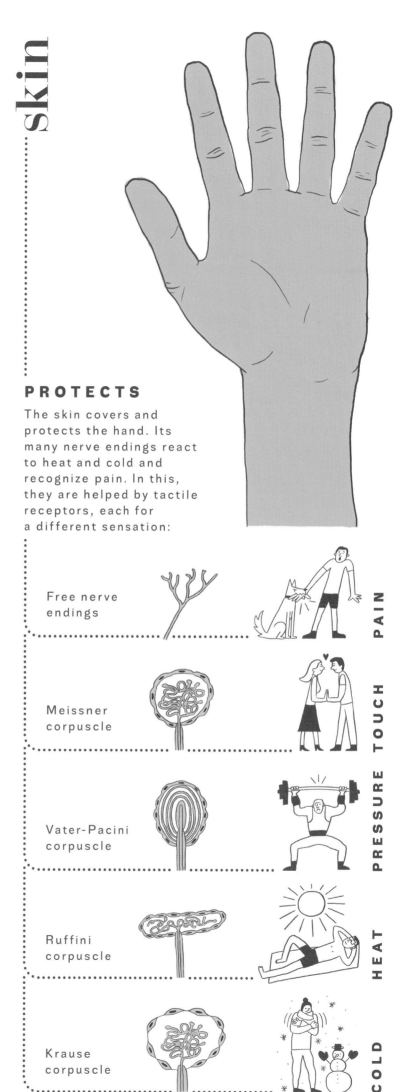

PROTECTS

The skin covers and protects the hand. Its many nerve endings react to heat and cold and recognize pain. In this, they are helped by tactile receptors, each for a different sensation:

Free nerve endings		PAIN
Meissner corpuscle		TOUCH
Vater-Pacini corpuscle		PRESSURE
Ruffini corpuscle		HEAT
Krause corpuscle		COLD

What is the best thing about hands?

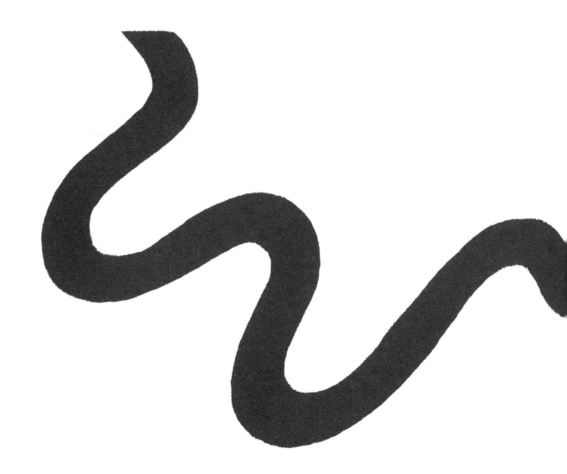

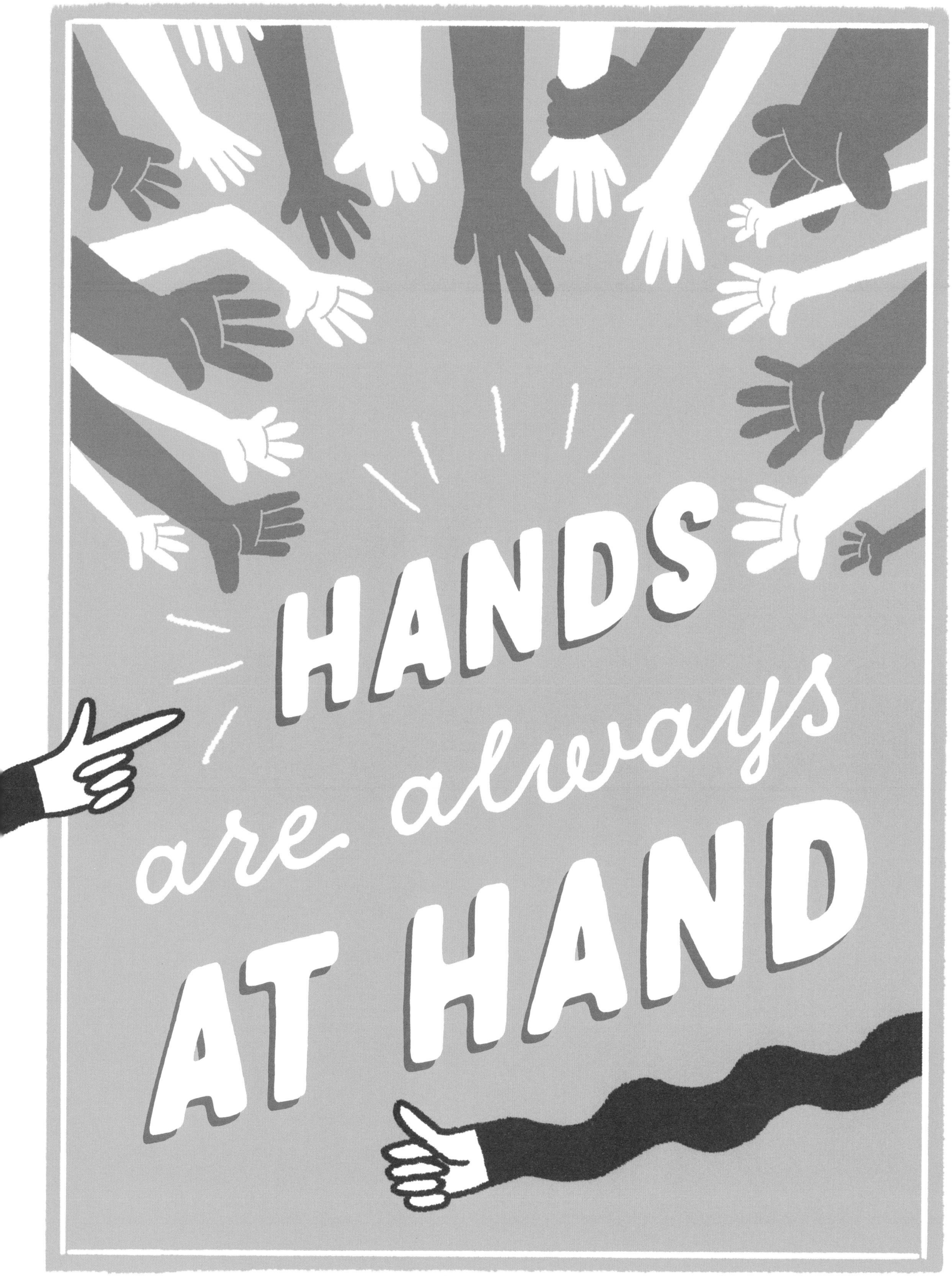
HANDS
are always
AT HAND

hold a large
mug of tea

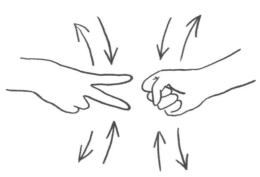

play rock,
paper, scissors

comb hair

pet hair

morph into
a wolf

What can

snap

make
pizza
dough

help a friend

knit

catch a thief   thieve

open a door

cup water

20

follow a map

perform a play

play the saxophone

hold up the world

a human hand do?

find the way in the dark

draw

box

swing from a tree

catch a ball

turn a page

Corner
TO BE CUT

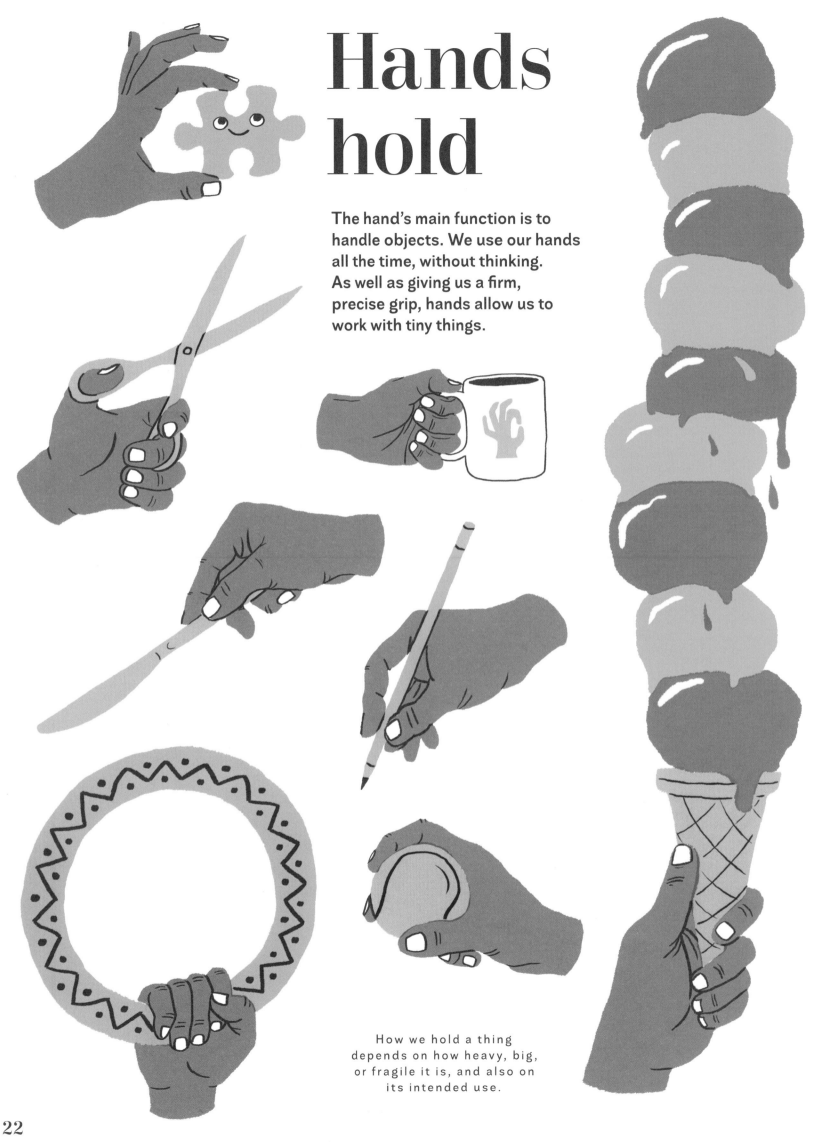

Hands hold

The hand's main function is to handle objects. We use our hands all the time, without thinking. As well as giving us a firm, precise grip, hands allow us to work with tiny things.

How we hold a thing depends on how heavy, big, or fragile it is, and also on its intended use.

give & cooperate

Hands sometimes need to cooperate. Why? Because one hand isn't always enough.

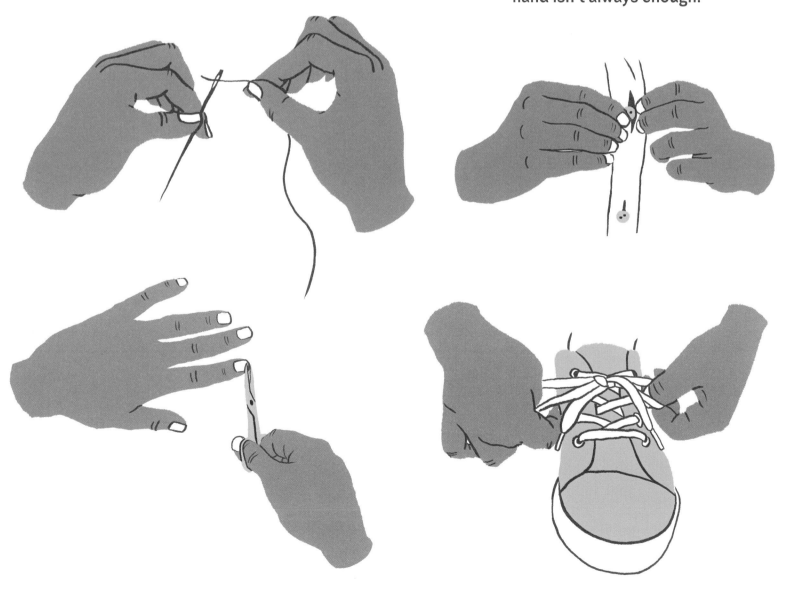

Hands are good for weightlifting. This demands very strong muscles.

THE HAND AS SUPPORT

We can lean against many things: a wall, another person, ski poles. We use this skill mostly when we're very young or old, when we are less stable.

rest

Our hands come in useful when we need to lean on or support something. When we fall, on instinct we hold out our hands.

For more **sticks** see pg. 68

TOUCH

We touch things and we touch each other. As touch is the 'first language' of life, parents take their baby in their arms straight after the birth.

There are touches of kindness—a mother's stroking hand or a hug from a friend, for instance.

& touch

But there are unkind touches too, like punching.

We perceive cold,
humidity, and heat
by touch.

THE HAND AS SENSOR

As well as being a protective cover for the body, the skin has a sensory function. Its nerves respond to stimuli in its surroundings. This is due to the important sense of touch, which sends signals to the brain via receptors and nerve endings. Because the fingertips have the most receptors, the hand is perfect for exploration and discovery.

feel & recognize

By touch, too, we recognize
the size, shape, and texture
of things. So we never
confuse a rabbit with a ball.

TOUCH

Touch is the first sense we develop in our mother's tummy. After sight, we rely on it more than any other sense.

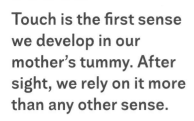

If you can't believe what you're seeing, **touch** it to make sure.

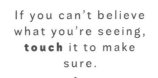

The hand feels pain, too. Ow! Don't get your fingers caught in a door or touch a hot stove!.

curiosity

9 out of **10** doctors recommend it.

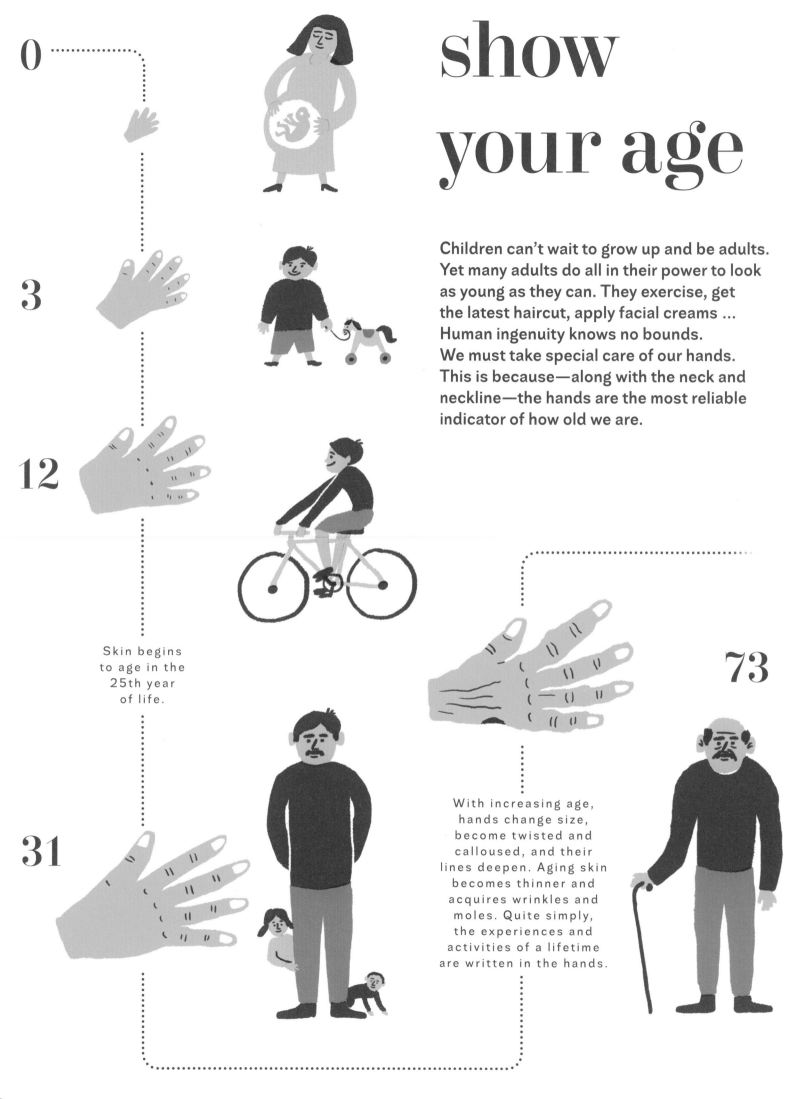

show your age

0

3

12

Skin begins
to age in the
25th year
of life.

31

Children can't wait to grow up and be adults. Yet many adults do all in their power to look as young as they can. They exercise, get the latest haircut, apply facial creams … Human ingenuity knows no bounds.
We must take special care of our hands. This is because—along with the neck and neckline—the hands are the most reliable indicator of how old we are.

73

With increasing age, hands change size, become twisted and calloused, and their lines deepen. Aging skin becomes thinner and acquires wrinkles and moles. Quite simply, the experiences and activities of a lifetime are written in the hands.

communicate

Communication is about sharing information and making ourselves understood. Without communication, the world would be in serious trouble. It may be a simple "hello"; it may be a long conversation with a friend.

VERBAL AND NONVERBAL COMMUNICATION

There are times when verbal communication (speech) isn't enough. Some things are hard to express in words. Sometimes we don't know what to say, so we search in vain for the right expression. Thank goodness for nonverbal communication! That's right: we can speak without words! A scratch of the forehead, a raising of the eyebrows, a smile, an outstretched tongue—all these are facial expressions. What can we express with the hands?

facial expression

Understanding verbal and nonverbal communication

words

gesture

stance

WHO SAYS MORE?

Which form of communication is best? To which do we pay most attention? Well, it depends on the situation. Sometimes words win out, sometimes a firm handshake does. Often, we communicate by a combination of the two.

Want to know how to communicate with your hands? Read on to find out.

We can ball our hands into fists, give a thumbs-up, or point: the meaning is clear without words. We understand many gestures intuitively, especially when they are supported by facial expressions. The best thing about them is clarity and straightforwardness.

speak

We perform countless gestures every day, consciously and unconsciously.

THE GREAT POWER OF GESTURES

Most gestures accompany speech. We often don't realize how much our hands are saying for us. As well as expressing emotion, they serve to emphasize and supplement our words. Sometimes they replace words entirely.

The legendary "'V' for victory" sign received a new lease on life from **Winston Churchill** in World War II. We still use it today.

Antiquity lived by gestures. It was one of the most important components of the art of rhetoric.

Quiet!

Speaker's gesture

Interesting.

Gesture of introduction

Excellent!

THE HISTORY OF THE GESTURE

The gesture is a tool of communication older than speech itself. We have been using it since prehistoric times. Gestures go through different phases. They get forgotten, then rediscovered.

Frequently used gestures

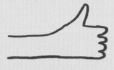

I LIKE IT

Thailand, Iraq

I DON'T LIKE IT. YUCK!

CALL ME, SURFERS' GESTURE

STOP

Greece

FORGET YOU!

whole world

V – GESTURE FOR PEACE OR VICTORY

with palm facing inward

Britain, Australia, New Zealand, Greece

COME HERE

Japan, Philippines

HOLDING YOUR THUMB

Pakistan

FINGERS CROSSED

Vietnam

O.K.
indicates money in Japan

Brazil, Turkey, France, Belgium, Tunisia

ROCKERS' GESTURE

Italy, Brazil, Cuba, Colombia, Portugal, Spain, Argentina

I + **Love** + **You** = **I LOVE YOU**

This gesture originated in sign language.

Many gestures work across cultures, all over the world. Like words, gestures can have multiple meanings, so we must use them with care.

make signals

What do we do if we find ourselves in a situation that demands that we keep our mouth zipped? Or if another person is too far away for our words to reach them?

Well, we use our hands. Apart from gesturing and fingerspelling, there are many codified signs for manual communication. They are used by professional and special groups where ordinary communication is impossible.

SEVERE CONDITIONS

When the recipient is far away or cannot speak

divers

signal flags – used at sea, in the mountains, and by scouts

sailors

STRATEGY

When you don't want to reveal my intentions, or you wish to go unnoticed

volleyball players

baseball players

soldiers

NAVIGATION AND ORGANIZATION

… in other situations

cyclists

soccer referees

traffic police

flight navigators

greet

The giving of the right hand accompanied by a verbal greeting—such as "Hello"—is one of our oldest, most widespread gestures worldwide. It expresses respect, friendship, and good intentions.

HISTORY OF THE HANDSHAKE

The handshake originated in prehistoric times. It showed the peaceful intentions of all involved by making clear that no one was holding a weapon. One use of the handshake nowadays is confirmation of an agreement.

Shaking hands in greeting first appeared in medieval Europe—allegedly because it would reveal hidden weapons in the sleeve.

Other greetings

The handshake is a widely practiced greeting. Even so, we shouldn't forget about cultural differences. Handshakes vary in strength and length. Should we make eye contact? Should we shake hands at all?

hongi (Māori)

kiss of the hand

bow
(Japanese)

wave

namaste (Hindu)

The right way to shake hands

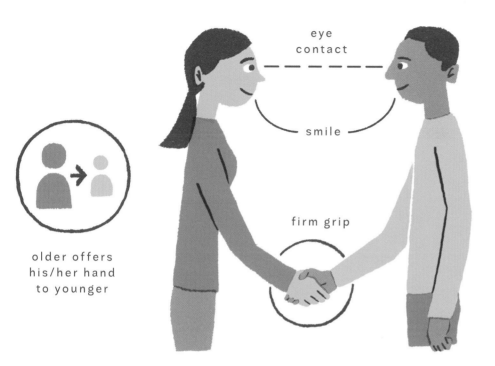

older offers
his/her hand
to younger

eye
contact

smile

firm grip

What not to do

- shake hands with a glove on
- offer a dirty hand

grip too hard

offer you hand
like a "limp fish."

salute (military)

high-five
(slapping palms)

"Live long
and prosper!"
(Star Trek)

fist bump

Scout's half-salute
(left-handed)

can replace eyes

Sight is our most important sense. We take in 80% of our information with our eyes. That's almost everything. But what if we can't see?

HANDS AS THE EYES OF THE VISUALLY IMPAIRED

Visually impaired people use their hands to read, recognize objects, even to form an idea of a friend's appearance. Hands help them enjoy art and games and make their way about the city.

We don't have a heightened sense of touch ...

Tactile signs and notices for the visually impaired are everywhere around us. Think of the guidelines and orientation points on pavements, and the Braille signs in elevators, on railings, next to monuments, and on boxes of medicine.

... but as we use it more, it becomes more sensitive.

Visually impaired people use everyday objects such as watches, remote controls, and board games. But they have them specially adapted.

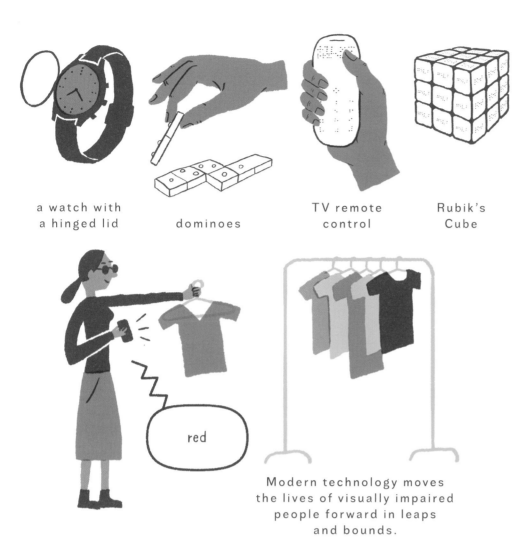

a watch with a hinged lid

dominoes

TV remote control

Rubik's Cube

red

Modern technology moves the lives of visually impaired people forward in leaps and bounds.

Visually impaired people often have long sticks and/or guide dogs. The stick checks the space around them, ensuring there is nothing in the way. A person with a white stick with red stripes is hearing and vision impaired.

Braille

1	2	3	4	5	6	7	8	9	0
a	b	c	d	e	f	g	h	i	j

k	l	m	n	o	p	q	r	s	t

u	v	w	x	y	z

?	!	dot	comma	captial letter	number

There is no unified Braille system—characters vary from country to country.

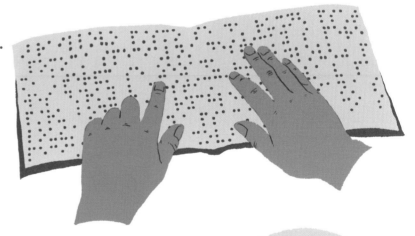

Visually impaired people have their own script, which, of course, they read by hand. It was created by Frenchman **Louis Braille**, who was blind himself. Cells comprise six dots arranged in a rectangle. Raised dots are perceived by touch. Every letter, number, or symbol has its own combination of raised points. That's the secret of Braille.

Louis Braille
(1809–1852)

can replace the ears & mouth

Deaf people use their hands to speak and even to hear. For this purpose, they invented not only fingerspelling but also a whole sign language.

Sign language

Individual words and phrases have their own special sign. Signs are expressed by specific hand positions and movements. Every little thing—the angle of the hands, the positioning and motions of the fingers—has its role. Question marks and exclamation marks are shown by facial expression and how the head and upper body are held.

IT'S RAINING

calm expression

slow downward motion of the hands

IT'S RAINING HEAVILY

dramatic expression

hand and finger movements are quicker, accelerating along with the rain's intensity

Be aware that like the spoken word, sign language varies from country to country.

WHAT IS YOUR NAME?

in British sign language

in American sign language

Fingerspelling

You don't have to be hearing impaired to know how to fingerspell. You can learn it before you go to school to keep your friends entertained in class.

One-handed fingerspelling is the most common worldwide. It looks like this:

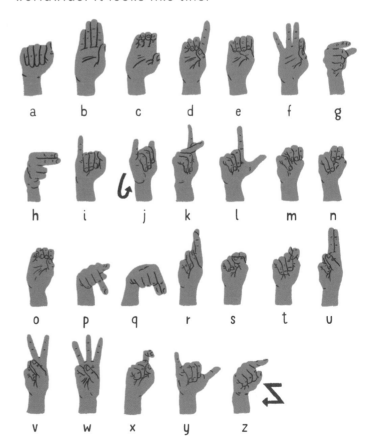

a b c d e f g

h i j k l m n

o p q r s t u

v w x y z

Deaf people communicate by sign language. Sign-language interpreters—you've probably seen them on TV, in a little box in the corner of the screen—help them make themselves understood.

Interpreters also assist deaf people when they see the doctor or are in the public space. They often interpret politicians' speeches and—and this is quite an experience!—rock concerts.

Famous *blind* & *deaf* people

Andrea Bocelli
(b.1958)
opera singer

Ray Charles
(1930–2004)
musician

Helean Keller
(1880–1968)
writer

Ludwig van Beethoven
(1770–1827)
composer

Thomas Alva Edison
(1847–1931)
inventor

Putting up a shelf, cooking lunch, sewing on a button, modeling a statue, building a wall, composing music—all are creative processes. And all need our hands.

create

Each activity makes different demands of our hands. A bricklayer's hands are strong. A sculptor's have a feel for shape, mass, and material. A composer's have agile fingers, ideally long ones.

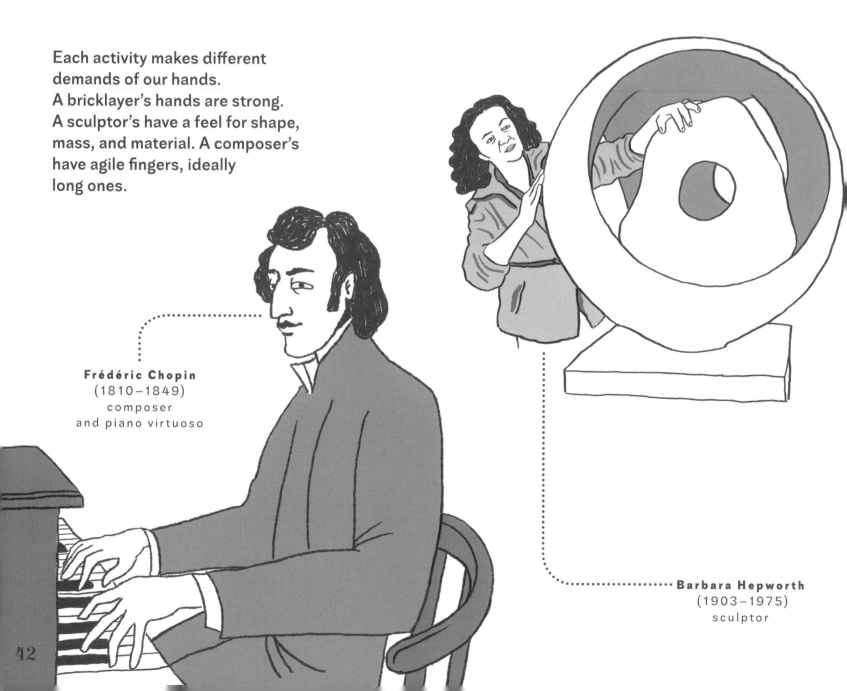

Frédéric Chopin
(1810–1849)
composer
and piano virtuoso

Barbara Hepworth
(1903–1975)
sculptor

Kurt Cobain
(1967–1994)
musician

& DESTROY

Pablo Picasso
painter

Clara Schumann
pianist and composer

Venus de Milo
statue

Famous hands

Makers of history, creators of supreme works, players in unforgettable events ... Happily, there are many inspirational, iconic figures. It's a pity so few of them can fit on one page.

Freddie Mercury
singer

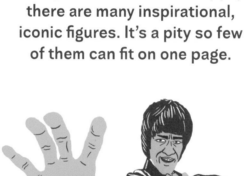

Bruce Lee
martial arts master and actor

Diego Maradona
footballer

Marina Abramović
artist

Amelia Earhart
pioneer of aviation

Herbert von Karajan
conductor

Václav Havel
Czech president

Tarzan
king of the jungle

Martina Navrátilová
tennis player

John Coltrane
jazz musician

Jane Goodall
scientist

Josef Sudek
photographer

Niccolò Paganini
violinist

Agatha Christie
writer

Buddha
Enlightened One

Marie Curie
physicist and chemist

Human hands are

Paws, fins, wings, tentacles, claws: these are the limbs of the animal kingdom. Few animals have hands as such. And most of them don't look much like our hands either. They work in so many different, fascinating ways!

dog

octopus

lion

penguin

cat

otter

elephant

bat

tarantula

squirrel

turtle

crab

sloth

camel

koala

chameleon

eagle

frog

stag beetle

kingfisher

ant

mouse

bear

platypus

cow

anteater

crocodile

46

unique in nature

bonobo   orangutan   chimpanzee   gorilla

Human hands closely resemble those of other apes.

Differences between human hands and other great ape hands

1. PROPORTIONS

The main difference is in the ratio of thumb to fingers. The human hand is more symmetrical; its palm and fingers are shorter and less curved. Other apes do not use their hands as humans do (see point 2).

2. USES

We have shown the range of things a human hand can do. Other apes need hands only for working with simple objects and when moving about (walking, climbing, hanging from trees). This explains why an ape's hands are stronger than a human's, with longer fingers. For dexterity, see point 3.

3. DEXTERITY

An ape's fingers can pluck tiny parasites from the coat of another ape. An ape can get at food by pushing a stick through a narrow opening. It has a firm grip and fine motor skills. Yet the human hand is way more dexterous and sensitive, largely due to the greater opposition of the human thumb, which can reach across the entire palm and to the fingertips. The human hand is broader in scope and more precise in its actions. It can arch the palm to pinch with all the fingers, which the ape's hand cannot.

The human hand is unique!

 **How did it come to be unique? Find out on the next page.**

47

The long journey toward hands

Humans developed into the creatures we are today over an unimaginably long time. This process is known as evolution—and it is worth a whole thick book of its own. But let's just cover the basics. Scientists tell us that life on Earth began 4 billion years ago, and that 3.6 billion of these years passed before the appearance of anything even vaguely resembling a hand.

The evolution of the hand in its current form occurred at the time of the first primates, taking over 60 million years. Several evolutionary changes contributed to this long and complex process. After all, evolution doesn't happen overnight.

Start

Planet Earth
is formed

the first **cells**

fish

3.6 billion years ago:
vertebrates reach land,
setting the stage for
the evolution
of the hand

quadrupeds

five-digit
limbs

mammals

apes
(chimpanzees, gorillas, orangutans)

- takes hold of food
- hand-eye coordination
- some claws turn into nails

Australopithecus
4.2 million years ago

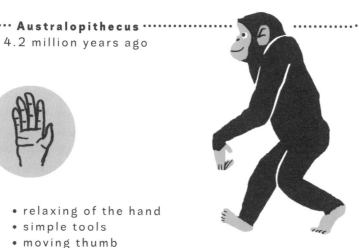

- firm grip
- simple tools
- hands used to move about
- partial thumb opposition
- nails
- allogrooming—caring for the coat and skin

- relaxing of the hand
- simple tools
- moving thumb
- shorter fingers

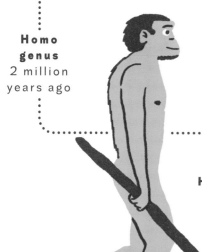

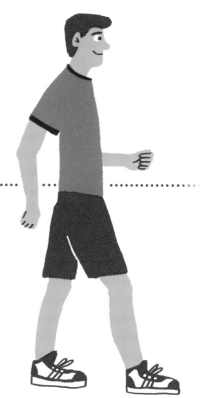

Homo genus
2 million years ago

Homo habilis
Homo ergaster
Homo erectus
Homo neanderthalensis

Homo sapiens sapiens – present day

- walking on two legs = hands free
- hands free = new possibilities
- nails = more sensitive, nimble fingers
- more dextrous hands = brain development
- gradual shortening of the palm brings thumb closer to fingers

THE WINNING HAND!

How do hands actually work?

Most workings of the body are governed by the brain. Body and brain are in constant communication. This fascinating collaboration happens at dizzying speeds. Without the brain, we couldn't move even a finger: every voluntary movement results from an electric impulse from the brain to the muscles.

> The hand is the visible part of the brain.

Immanuel Kant
(1724–1804)
philosopher

Hand movement is managed by thought. The hand makes thought material. The architect **Frank O. Gehry** used his hands intuitively to model a house from pieces of paper.

The endbrain has two **hemispheres**, each controlling one side of the body and its different functions. The **little brain** coordinates movement; without it, our movements would be jerky and robotic.

The little brain is at the back

In the brain, we find the whole person. We refer to it as the **homonucleus**—and there are two of them. That's because each side of the body is governed by a different part of the cerebral cortex. These homunculi—one sensory, the other motor—show how we would look if parts of the body grew as the cerebral cortex told them to. In both cases, the hand is the undisputed winner.

When the **sensory homonucleus** and the **motor homonucleus** come together

"I'm a right-hander, Mom. Come to the other side."

"I don't know which I am yet."

Left & right

We learn as small children which of our hands is defter. We use it more often, pick things up with it without thinking, write ... The dominance of one hand over the other is known as laterality.

Whether a child will be right- or left-handed is decided in the mother's tummy. But we won't know for sure which hand is predominant until he or she is at least one year old. Sometimes it only becomes clear when the child starts school.

left

9%
of people

Although left-handers have lots of minor inconveniences to deal with, left-handedness has its advantages too. It is said that left-handers are more creative and have better spatial perception. The moment of surprise is also in their favor—in sports and also in conquering a medieval castle.

Castle staircases ran clockwise—thus favoring defenders over would-be conquerors, as most people are right-handed. Of course, a clockwise staircase was no help against a left-handed invader.

FAMOUS LEFT-HANDERS

Julius Caesar
Charlie Chaplin
Isaac Newton
Johann Sebastian Bach
Franz Kafka
Václav Havel
Martina Navrátilová
Lady Gaga
David Bowie

Jimi Hendrix .... Robert de Niro .... Alexander the Great .... Queen Victoria .... Wolfgang Amadeus Mozart ....

ambidexterity

Strange as it may seem, some of us use both hands equally well. These people are ambidextrous.

1%
of people

Michelangelo painting
the Sistine Chapel

FAMOUS ABMIDEXTROUS PEOPLE

Leonardo da Vinci
Tapio Wirkkala
Keanu Reeves

Most people are better with their right hand—which explains why most objects and instruments (musical instruments, appliances, tools, etc.) are made for right-handers. What this means for left-handers you will find out on the next page ...

right

90%
of people

FAMOUS RIGHT-HANDERS

There are too many of them to list!

The left hand in trouble

Is one hand better than the other? Of course not. But all of us favor one hand over the other.

Even so, the left hand has a harder time. It was once thought of as worse and weaker, and also as unclean. The right hand was associated with reason, order, and logic.

Some cultures still view the left hand in negative terms—a fact of which we should be aware in India, the Arab world, and North Africa, for instance. Until the late 1960s, in some countries it was common for left-handers to be converted to right-handers. Fortunately, this is no longer done.

Competing hands in history

stupid

devilish

rational

clever

unclean

clean

clumsy

LEFT vs RIGHT

skillful

A computer's mouse is always on the wrong side.

Elbows of left-handers are forever poking people.

International Lefthanders Day

13 August

Use of right-handed tools is a pain for left-handers...

... and it may even be dangerous.

Most things are the wrong way around, including soup ladles.

Most things are made for right-handers.

The left-handed writer can have difficulty.

Hello. Do you sell left-handed scissors?

We did have some five years ago.

Fortunately, most everyday objects are made in left-handed versions today. We find them at specialist shops.

20th-century writer

21st-century writer

farmer

surgeon

Hands by profession

19th-century writer

manager

It is said that you can tell a lot about a person by their hands, including their profession. While a farmer is not afraid to get her hands dirty, a doctor is forever washing hers. A blacksmith grips his hammer tight, while a florist must handle his flowers gently. The work we do forms our hands by causing them to adapt.

architect

blacksmith

reader

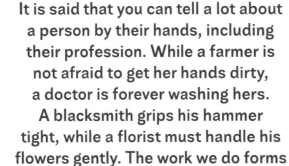

hairdresser

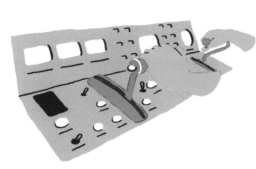

tram driver

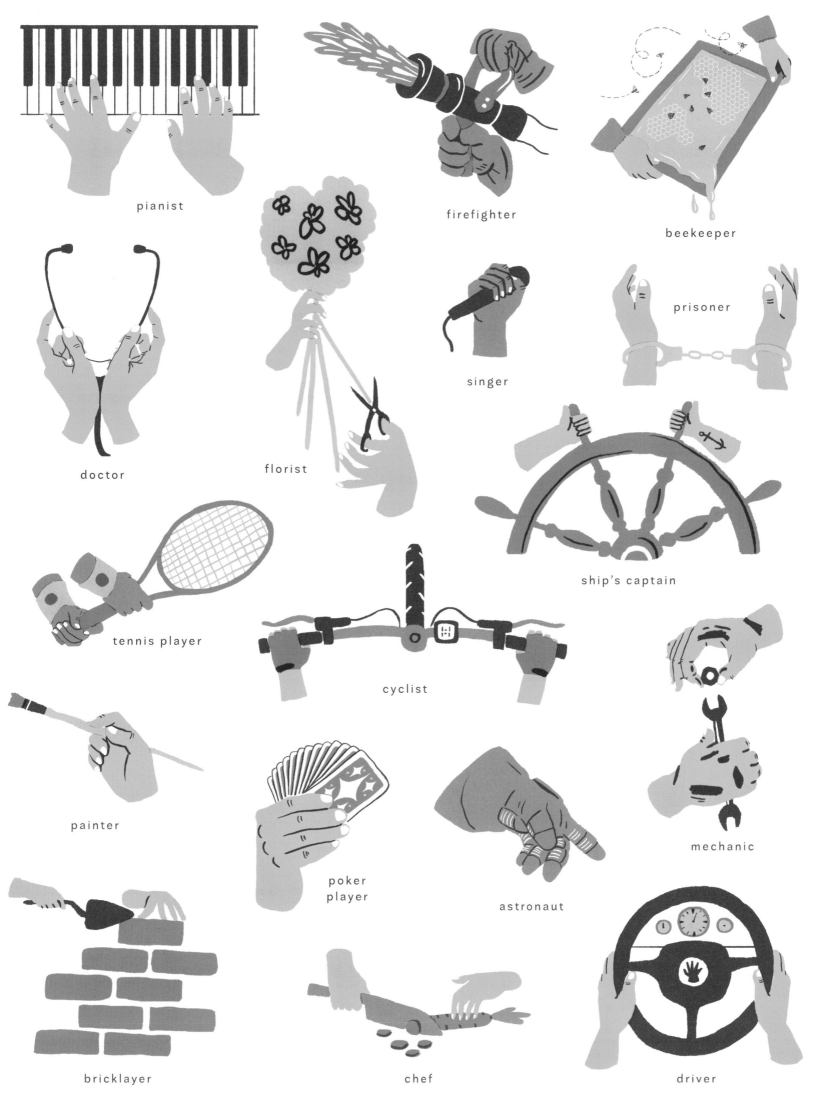

pianist

firefighter

beekeeper

doctor

florist

singer

prisoner

tennis player

ship's captain

cyclist

painter

poker player

astronaut

mechanic

bricklayer

chef

driver

Measuring with hands

It isn't really surprising. The hand (like other parts of the body) is great for measuring. How do we demonstrate that something is ‹— *this* big —›? We use our hands, of course. And we have done it that way since ancient times.

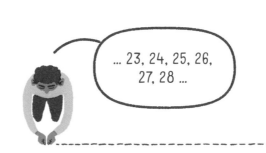

... 23, 24, 25, 26, 27, 28 ...

The oldest units of length were based on the size of different parts of the body—most commonly the hands, arms, and feet. All these units had names. The meaning of "foot" is clear. But what about span, yard, and inch?

Measurements in history

HAND

Popular from ancient times on, it equaled the width of the palm including the thumb. It was eventually fixed at **4 inches**. The hand is still used for measuring the height of horses.

YARD

This old British unit equals the distance from the tip of the nose to the tip of the middle finger of King Henry I's outstretched arm—**3 feet**. It's still used to measure football fields in many countries.

INCH

This once very popular unit of length was based on the width of a man's thumb. It varied from country to country, even between cities. It was eventually agreed that an inch equalled **25.4 mm**. Indicated by two vertical lines ("), it is used everywhere in America—like when we are buying a cell phone, TV, or car tire.

SPAN

Based on the width of the outstretched hand. Measurements can be made with both hands—either two hands side by side, or one hand from thumb to pinky.

CUBIT

One of the oldest measurements of length, it was used from ancient times until the 19th century, when metric units were introduced.

A ruler you always have on you

- Measure your hand in all possible and impossible ways.
- Remember the measurements.
- If you are still growing, update the measurements regularly.
- Use your hand instead of a ruler.

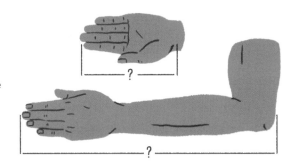

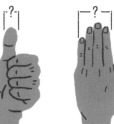

Tip: Knowledge of hand size helps when buying gloves. See pg. 67

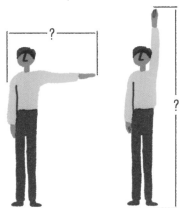

Measure your feet too, even though they are not hands. This will come in handy.

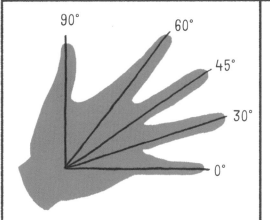

90° 60° 45° 30° 0°

Tip: You can use your hand as a protractor, too.

How we count on our fingers differs between countries.

Europe

United States, Britain, China

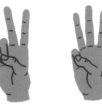

Japan

1   2   3   4   5

Hands are symbols

As the hand is amazing, practical, and known by all, it is no wonder people have long used it as a symbol—a representative of deeper meaning. In many cultures, it is used to mean the same thing. It often symbolizes the hand of God, protection, life, or might.

Rule & power

The hand is a traditional symbol of strength (or of the threat of strength) and the power and rule that goes with it. The motif of the hand is often found in heraldry, especially in the coats of arms of cities and families. It has been a common motif on scepters and other staffs of authority since ancient times.

Prague coat of arms

scepter of French kings

Red Hand of Ulster: symbol of the province in Ireland

advocate's staff

HAMSA

The hamsa is a palm-shaped amulet often seen on jewelry and wall decorations. It protects the wearer or dwelling from evil forces. It is important to the Islamic and Jewish faiths. Muslims refer to it as the Hand of Fatima, Jews as the Hand of Miriam. Its purpose remains the same.

These amulets are said to provide protection against the evil eye—hence the eye symbol.

Blessing

HAND OF GOD

The Hand of God can take many forms. In most cases, it symbolizes calmness and security—in short, everlasting care and protection.

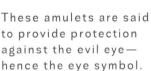

Jesus Christ giving a blessing

The blessing hands of the Kohanim is a common motif on Jewish gravestones.

Abhayamudra—gesture of the Buddha's protection of all living beings

There is much more, of course. But we have run out of space.

Depictions of hands

Hands are loved by artists from many different cultures and time periods. Ordinary and unique, hands are rich in symbols, unchanging, and universal. An ideal theme.

Hands of the Chimú culture, Peru, 9th–15th century

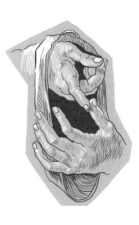

Albrecht Dürer, *Study of Hands*, 1506

Edvard Munch, *The Scream*, detail, 1893

Vidal Mayor, manuscript, detail, 1290

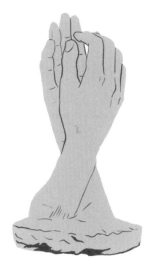

Auguste Rodin, *The Cathedral*, 1908

Yves Klein, *Untitled*, 1962

Fragment of a royal hand, Egypt, c. 1350 BCE

Statue fragment, Ancient Greece, 1st century BCE

Katsushika Hokusai, *Girl with Flower*, 1802

Figure, Wari culture, Peru, 9th–15th century

Pablo Picasso, *Guernica*, detail, 1937

Figurine of the Mambila tribe, Nigeria, 19th–20th century

Max Beckmann, *The Old Actress*, detail, 1926

Guidonian Hand, manuscript, detail, 1274

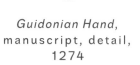

Frans Hals, *Portrait of a Woman*, detail, 1627

Thumbs up!

César Baldaccini, *Thumb*, 1965

Damien Hirst,
Hands in Prayer,
2017

Cave of Hands, detail, Argentina,
c. 7,000–11,000 BCE

Nefertiti and Akhenaten,
fragment, Egypt,
c. 1350 BCE

Goddess Durga,
India, 20th century

Toyen,
A Sad Day, detail,
1942

Leonardo da Vinci,
Mona Lisa, detail,
1503–1506

Hands,
Villanovan culture,
7th century BCE

**Mierle Laderman
Ukeles**,
Touch Sanitation,
performance,
1977–1980

El Greco,
*The Knight with His Hand
on His Breast*,
1580

**Alberto
Giacometti**,
The Hand,
1947

Egon Schiele,
Self-portrait,
detail,
1910

**Gian Lorenzo
Bernini**,
*The Rape of
Proserpina*, detail,
1621–1622

Vincent van Gogh,
Old Man in Sorrow, detail
1890

**Michelangelo
Buonarroti**,
David, detail,
1501–1504

Andrei Rublev,
St John the Baptist,
15th century

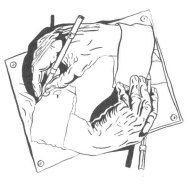

Caravaggio,
The Calling of St Matthew, detail,
1599–1600

**Marina Abramović
and Ulay**,
Point of Contact,
1980

Lorenzo Quinn,
Support, 2017

M. C. Escher,
Drawing Hands,
1948

Hand decorations

nail of
a Babylonian
warrior

henna
nail polish
from Ancient
India and
Egypt

decorative
nail extension,
China

Inca
nail

People have always decorated their bodies—including their hands. Tattooing, body-painting with henna and nail-coloring have been worldwide phenomena for over 5,000 years.

Won't you paint my nails instead?

Nail-coloring

Nail-coloring really took off in the 20th century.

1917 – first nail varnish

1930s – iconic red nails popularized by Rita Hayworth

1970s – French manicures

1957 – false fingernail

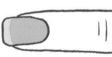

modern times – glitter nail varnish

pebble nail varnish

very long false nail with colorful motif

nail filed into an almond shape

nail filed into a square shape

Skin dyeing

The motifs we adorn our bodies with may be abstract, realistic, or ornamental. **Henna** or **tattoo**? Well, the former is temporary (a natural dye, it lasts only a few days), the latter permanent. A tattoo is made by injecting a colored pigment under the skin. Tattoos can be removed only deliberately, by a laser procedure.

Rings & accessories

Rings. We may be struck by their shine, but they are not mere ornaments. Indeed, most rings have a deeper meaning. As it begins and ends nowhere, the ring symbolizes eternity and infinity, and often commitment. It is worn by old ladies, nobility, and church dignitaries, and even by hard-edged rockers.

ring of office
in the past symbolized the office of a monarch, bishop, or other authority

family ring
heirloom (passed from one generation to the next)

magical ring
its magic powers may help or harm

wooden ring
a ring made of non-conducting material, suitable for electricians

ornamental ring
has no symbolic meaning, comes in a wide range of shapes and designs

Prometheus ring
in legend, the world's first ring, forged from Prometheus's chain in the Caucasus Mountains

ring with gemstone
a popular type, with a wide range of colors and designs

member's ring
shows membership of a club, association, or university graduation

fan
for fanning the face on hot summer's days

ring with a secret compartment
for concealing a message or poison

signet ring
used mainly in the past, for the authentication of documents

wedding and engagement ring
used to confirm the marriage vow and symbolize everlasting love

thumb ring
of bold design – for extroverts

bracelets
of various types and materials, with or without a charm, symbolic or purely ornamental

watch
used to show the time, it is worn to ensure we are never late

Gloves

Gloves were first worn in ancient times. Although they were decorative and were signs of prestige, their main function was protection—as it still is today. Gloves protect the wearer or what the wearer touches. They keep out winter cold, dampen hammer blows, and make cleaning the toilet easier. Formal gloves can look really smart too.

For keeping warm

mittens (knitted)

gloves with fingers (knitted)

waterproof gloves

leather gloves

gloves with overlay

fingerless gloves

gloves with strings

Formal gloves

gentlemen's

lace

ladies'

For sport

ski

cycling

goalkeeper

baseball

golf

boxing

Work gloves

rubber

medical

work

kitchen

gardening (with claws)

museum staff

Special

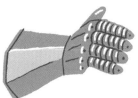
knight's

grilling

driver's

superhero's

biker's

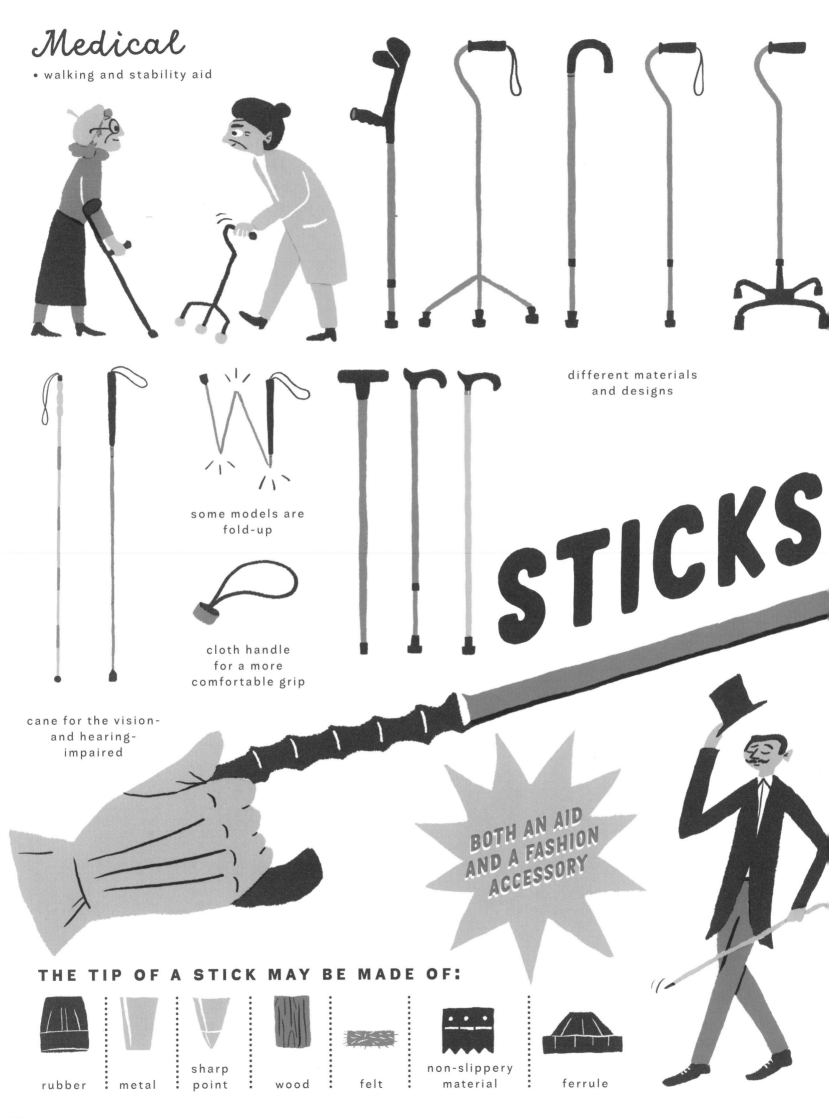

Medical

- walking and stability aid

different materials
and designs

some models are
fold-up

cloth handle
for a more
comfortable grip

cane for the vision-
and hearing-
impaired

STICKS

BOTH AN AID
AND A FASHION
ACCESSORY

THE TIP OF A STICK MAY BE MADE OF:

rubber : metal : sharp point : wood : felt : non-slippery material : ferrule

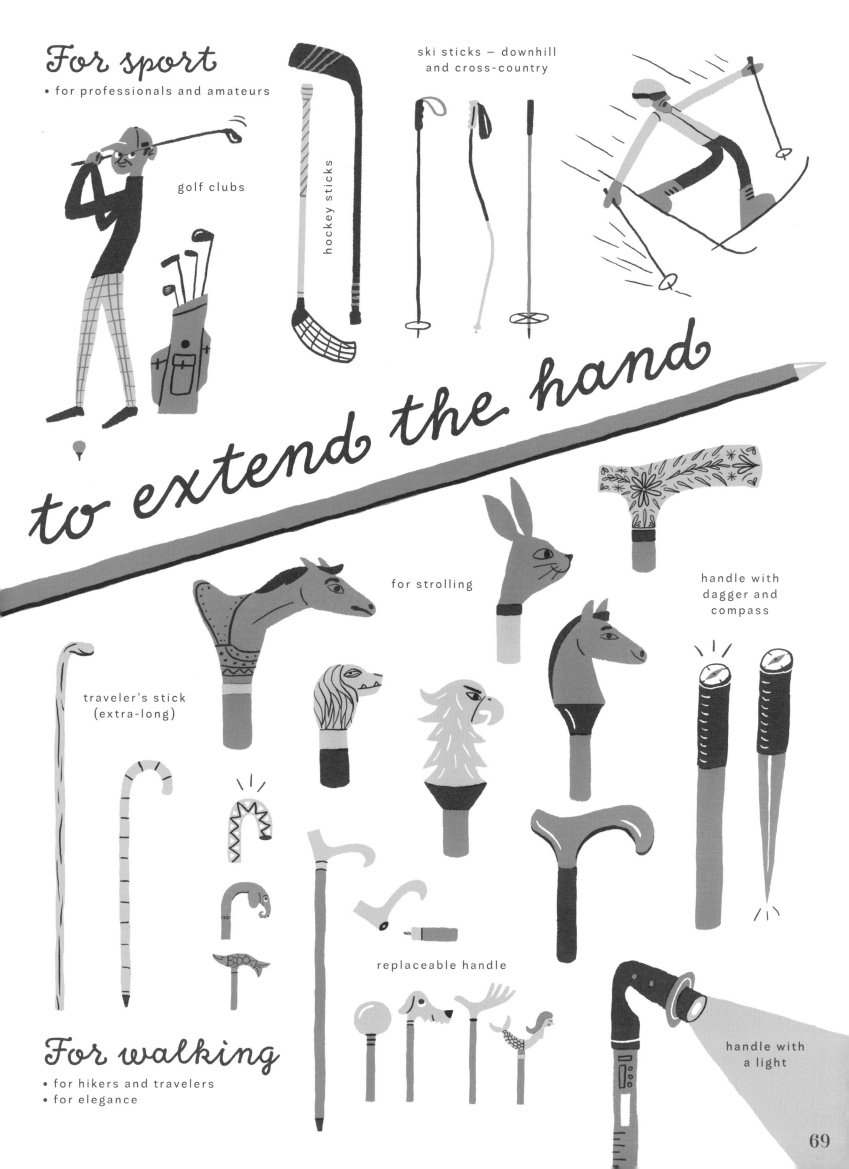

For sport

- for professionals and amateurs

golf clubs

hockey sticks

ski sticks – downhill and cross-country

to extend the hand

for strolling

handle with dagger and compass

traveler's stick (extra-long)

replaceable handle

For walking

- for hikers and travelers
- for elegance

handle with a light

Injured hands

An injured hand is a troublesome thing. Even a small hand injury can make life difficult. We should take care to protect our hands.

The hand can be affected by a number of problems. While little scratches or bruises are hardly worth mentioning, other complaints can be a real bother, requiring long, demanding treatment.*

alien hand syndrome

severed finger

hypermobility

cut hand

amputated fingers

burns

excessive sweating

scars

ripped-off nail

loss of a hand

carpal tunnel inflammation

arthritis

rash

dislocation

bone fracture

swelling

* If you have a problem, see a doctor.

At the doctor's

A sick hand needs treatment. Before this can start, a diagnosis must be made. Specialist doctors help us solve all kinds of problems with our health.

The doctor first examines the hand by sight and touch, or by using instruments for an X-ray or ultrasound examination. Alternative medicine treatments, such as acupuncture, reflexology, or herbal remedies, are also possible.

general practitioner
treats minor injuries and refers patients to specialists

orthopedist
resets dislocated shoulders and fingers

prosthetist
chooses the right artificial hand for you

neurologist
treats numb hands

surgeon
repairs the inside of the hand

dermatologist
rids you of rashes and warts

rheumatologist
treats aching joints

plastic surgeon
smooths away scars

A typical hand injury and its treatment

bone fracture (over time):

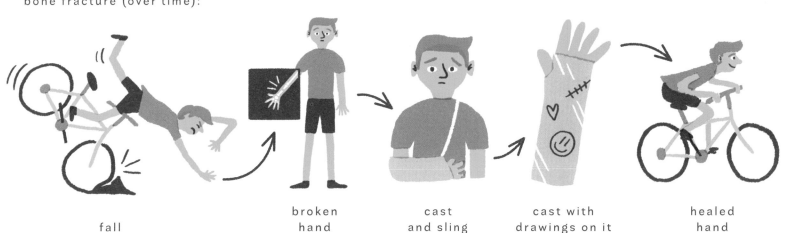

fall

broken hand

cast and sling

cast with drawings on it

healed hand

The way to A REPLACEMENT HAND

People have always contended with the loss of limbs as a result of accident, illness, or war, so there has long been a need for a replacement—known as a prosthesis.

HANDS are a TREASURE

Try not to injure them!

Take good care of them!

Protect them from cold and direct sunlight!

Hand hygiene

These days we wash our hands as a matter of course, but this wasn't always so. Incredible though it now seems, in the early 19th century, doctors and nurses ridiculed the idea of handwashing. We owe the change in behavior to the installation of water mains, the building of sewers, the development of soap, and the work of visionaries such as Ignaz Semmelweis and Louis Pasteur. Semmelweis insisted that doctors wash their hands to prevent the spread of infectious disease, while Pasteur helped detect microbial agents of infection.

Beware of microbes!

Louis Pasteur
(1822–1895)

Please wash your hands.

Ignaz Semmelweis
(1818–1865)

The dirtiest things

A cell phone is far dirtier than a toilet seat.

cell phone

keyboard & remote control

kitchen sponge

door handle

dog toy

money and wallet

elevator & ATM buttons

shopping trolley & basket

HARSH STATISTICS

- 80% of diseases are transmitted by touch.
- Only 5% of people wash their hands properly.
- Most people wash their hands for only 6 seconds.
- Damp hands spread bacteria 1,000 times easier than dry hands.
- Only 20% of people dry their hands after washing.
- Bacteria thrives under jewelry—before handwashing, it is important to remove rings.
- A banknote contains between 50 and 48,000 bacteria.

How to wash hands

Handwashing should last at least **40 seconds**.

Wet your hands.

Apply soap.

In a circular motion, spread the soap across the palms, the backs of the hands, and between the fingers...

...not forgetting the thumbs and nails.

Rinse your hands.

Dry them.

Now your hands are clean!

stick them into
a lion's cage (or other
inappropriate places)

bang your
fists on the
table

What not to do with hands

pet
a cactus

bite your
nails

make
inappropriate
gestures

pick your
nose

wipe your plate
with a finger

work without protective gloves

steal stuff

touch valuable museum exhibits

ring a stranger's doorbell for fun

torment animals

lick dirty fingers

PROTECT HANDS IN WINTER

Marcel Duchamp 1964

with gloves!

The Hand book

© Designed by B4U Publishing for Albatros,
an imprint of Albatros Media Group, 2022
5. května 1746/22, Prague 4, Czech Republic
Author: Magda Garguláková, Illustrator: Vítězslav Mecner
Translator: Andrew Oakland, Editor: Scott Alexander Jones
Printed in China by Asia Pacific

ISBN: 978-80-00-06600-4